Li Rainbows

A Book About Auras

Published by
Light Technology Publishing
Sedona, AZ

By
Gabriel Hudson Bain

Copyright 1993 Gabriel Hudson Bain

All rights reserved. No part of this book may be reproduced or transmitted in any form or by any means, electronic or mechanical, including photocopying, recording or by any informational storage or retrieval system -- except by a reviewer who may quote brief passages in a review to be printed in a magazine or newspaper -- without permission in writing from the publisher. For information contact

Published by
Light Technology Publishing
P.O. Box 1526
Sedona, AZ 86339
(602)282-6523
ISBN 0-929385-42-X

Cover Art: Watercolor by Mercedes White
Book Illustrations: Pen and Ink by Michael Cantrell
Portrait of the Author: Oil Pastel by
Mary Meyers-Cutsinger

Printed by
Mission Possible Printing
P.O. Box 1495
Sedona, AZ 86339
(602) 282-6523

THIS BOOK IS SPIRAL BOUND
FOR YOUR CONVENIENCE

CONTENTS

— CONTENTS —

PREFACE

This workbook was designed to share the techniques and exercises that will empower you to see and experience the aura in the simplest manner possible. In my workshops and seminars, this program has proven itself time and again to benefit those who have desired to see auras but haven't found the keys.

The keys to experiencing auras come one step at a time so please try not to be too anxious. I've watched my progress take place over the last 20 years. My ability has grown from seeing surface reactions to much more in-depth views.

Because of my great enjoyment in having this ability with auras, I wanted to share the ideas that I have learned and experienced. This book presents the teachings that I have been given over those years, as well as my experiences while working with the aura.

With thanks to: Diane Dudley, Lucy Stern, Jim Watson, MaryAnn Ashcroft, Patricia Bain, and Faye Tabor without whose help and inspiration this book would be far from what it is, a very satisfying endeavor.

I hope you enjoy many good years of benefits from this book.

Gabriel Hudson Bain

Introduction

What is an Aura?

WHAT IS AN AURA?

The aura is the result of the energy we radiate from our feelings, thoughts, and physical being. It can be seen as a bubble of light and color surrounding the body. The existence of auras is both fascinating and real. Most of us are unaware of them, yet in reality, they are as real as you and I.

For a moment, OPEN YOUR MIND ... open your mind to the possibility that people create auras. We create them by projecting energy from our bodies. All living things (plants and animals, too) have an aura, and we can sense and see them also.

You've sensed, through what we know as sixth sense, a person's aura when you felt his depression. You've sensed a person's aura when you felt his positive, radiant energy. Being aware of what you've sensed is feeling the aura, sort of a gut knowing. To see an aura is different. It takes applying your imagination, forgetting old ideas that say you can't, and letting this dormant ability that is alive within you right now become a useful tool.

Here is a little exercise that will allow you to become aware of what your aura sense is all about and it's as simple as visualizing an apple.

With your mind's eye, visualize an apple. See it sitting in front of you at arm's reach on a cutting board. There is a knife beside it. Now, imagine cool drops of water on the apple and "feel" the moisture.

Pick up the knife and cut the apple in two, hearing the knife cut through the apple striking the cutting board with a whack. Smell the fragrance that comes floating up from the apple. Pick up one half and bite into it. Let the juices make your mouth water, and if it's sour or sweet let that expression happen also.

The real wonder of this ability to see and sense the apple is fascinating. It requires applying your imagination and your inner senses to experience the apple off in the corner of the mind, not as directly looking at it, but envisioning it softly out there. In the same degree, this is how you will see the aura in the beginning, off in the corner of your mind.

Notice how you were able to visualize the apple simply and quickly. This was mainly because it posed no threat to you or to your imagination. You played a little game with your mind and used an object that is familiar. When the mind or subconscious does not feel threatened, it allows itself to work freely with suggestions given to it. That is what it takes to begin to see auras. It's a playful, non-threatening game.

How can we begin to see or recognize something if we don't know what it looks like? With the help of some illustrations in this book, you will be on your way to seeing and sensing auras in no time at all.

Once you understand the principles and the basics of aura energies, the rest will come naturally. As we go through this material, I'll work with you just as I work with people in my aura workshops, which is to say that I'll introduce ideas to you in that form. I have discovered that when approaching auras in this order, I seem to have the best results.

I want you to s-t-r-e-t-c-h your imagination and really play with this. The more fun you have doing it without being too serious about it, the faster your awareness will open up.

All of your life you've recognized and talked about the aura, you just didn't realize it. This is what you were talking about when you used phrases like "Red with anger, feeling blue, in the pink, getting the cold shoulder, and turning green with envy."

These sayings do have a realness about them that is fascinating. Perhaps you feel that you can sense auras, but that you can't see them. Contrary to popular sentiment, the aura can be easily seen once you develop your inner-sensing and imagination. TRUST IN YOURSELF. You can accomplish this through practice.

As an infant when you had no other way of communicating with your new reality, you used an inherent ability to sense and relate information to yourself. Then as you developed more physical abilities, this inner-sense moved into the background. This sense still works, however, every moment of everyday. By paying attention to ideas, feelings, inspiration, and cues from the world, you will soon become more aware of this ability.

The mind is complex in the way it receives and stores information. There are a hundred and one things occurring to your senses every moment of your life. Consciously, there is no way you could keep up with all the information your Being is receiving. Your everyday mind would overload. So, life gave you the ability to sort it out and focus on what you consider to be the most important area for the moment: working, talking, exercising, or meditating.

You were given an inner, psychic self that quietly and constantly goes about its business distributing information to areas of the mind for storage or activation, while retaining the ability to bring to the front of your mind whatever you need, whenever you need it. This includes anything from dealing with emergencies to remembering a name.

Have you ever followed a thought? And have you seen how many memories are connected to one thing? Memory storage is based on the amount of emotional energy surrounding the in-coming information. If the material is highly charged, it can spring to your mind instantly. If not, it requires more work or searching in your mind. But you can always remember your past.

Now at this point you are probably wondering what this has to do with auras? Well, subconsciously you see auras but you don't give them validity unless they are unusual.

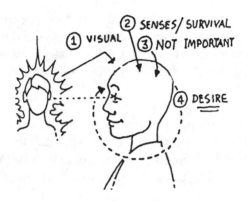

The inner, psychic self sorting information.

When you receive aura information, your psychic-self shoves it into the background so you can pay attention to where your interest is centered. Usually, and this deals with your everyday meeting with others, it's involved in the conversation or the looks of the person and not with what is happening on the other levels, i.e., I'm thinking about what she's thinking and about what to do or say next, and all sorts of other things, but not looking at the aura.

By seeing the aura, I can get a much more in-depth view of what is taking place and how I'm being perceived by the other person. And by knowing about remembering the past, I can look back, in my mind, and replay the event. In the replay I can now include the aura. You can learn to do this also.

How can you bring this ability into a more prominent role in your life? You begin to practice and focus your desire towards it. You start to refocus the incoming information by placing auras higher on the list of priorities and by paying more attention to them.

The techniques presented in this workbook are both ancient and new. They are designed especially for the development of aura sight. You might also want to include the questions at the end of this book to help expand your awareness and talent.

As most of you understand, this is an important time in the evolution of the human race. The evolution lies within the consciousness. Because of this raising of consciousness, each of us will encounter new aspects of ourselves. Part of this will include a new awareness of our inner-psyche, the sixth sense. With the sixth sense, we will encounter extra sight and extra feelings as well as seeing and feeling the Vibrations/Auras of people we know and people we don't. We will know how others feel being around us and how they are managing their thoughts of us or others. We will begin to see higher vibrating energies, things that are normally invisible to us. This is a natural happening for the human race and that's why I believe you will be successful with this material.

```
┌─────────────────────────────────┐
│          SECTION ONE            │
│   EXPERIENCING THE HUMAN AURA   │
└─────────────────────────────────┘
```

SANTA CRUZ , CA CIRCA 1974

THE FOUR SYMBOLS

VISUALIZING

LEVELS OF THE AURA

HOW TO SEE THE AURA

HOW TO SEE YOUR OWN

IS IT ETHICAL TO LOOK AT SOMEONE'S AURA?

THE FOUR STAGES OF AURA DEVELOPMENT

SANTA CRUZ, CA CIRCA 1974

In the small living room, we began our group lessons. We sat in a half-circle in front of Diane and waited with expectancy. A few candles were burning giving the room a soft, dim light.

"Good evening," began the Doctor. "Good evening," we replied. (The Doctor is Chinese and a Spirit. He is a higher aspect of my good friend Diane.)

"Let us begin with a short meditation of breathing and then we will discuss your first lesson." After calming ourselves, the Doctor continued.

Sitting cross-legged on a pillow, Diane looked comfortable, but her presence was missing from the room. The Doctor manipulated her body very easily. He placed the left hand on the left knee and held up the right hand with the palm facing towards the center of the circle.

"Do you see the energy coming from the hand?" We sat quietly and in awe. This was a new experience for us and because we didn't see the energy, we weren't confident enough to volunteer any answers.

There was a short pause. The Doctor smiled and said, "No? Well, please relax, and concentrate as we fill the room with Lavender light. This light will increase the vibrations allowing your physical eyes to tune in to the energies."

The Doctor closed the open palm of the right hand and then opened it again extending it back towards the group in a soft pushing motion. "What color do you feel?" I began to sense a difference in the room. My mind said 'yellow', so I said what I felt.

"Very good," replied the Doctor. Looking around the group, he directed his attention to another, "And what do you feel?" The session continued as the Doctor worked with each person in the group.

The first session was only 20 minutes long but very stimulating and we were all very excited. We talked a lot about what we experienced and we were anxious to have another session.

The Doctor taught us a lot about energies and auras and performed many experiments. The group gained an added awareness on Enlightenment and Universal Principles. It was a very exciting time in my life and I know it was for the others, too.

I had so much fun experiencing the group sessions that I wanted to share with you some of the events that happened in them. I also wanted to make sure this area was included in this book. I believe this helps bring things to a more personal level and it gives you the benefit of my mistakes and experiences, as well as the opportunity to try different techniques that were discovered along the way.

I will say that there was always room for the skeptic in me to surface and I did question what the spirit teacher taught to the group, from time to time.

After leaving the group I continued my studies and searched for other teachings that would match up with what we had been taught.

I found similarities in different subjects, was fascinated by Jane Robert's books on Seth, read about the discoveries of western physicists in relation to light frequencies, divine creation, and the stuff that forms matter. I read Carlos Castanada's books and other native teachings from around the world to see how those ideas matched with what I was learning and covered as many areas as I could that talked about spiritual awareness and manipulating energy.

Through all the years of study and working with people and their concepts of life, I have endeavored to communicate this information in the most sensible and reasonable way, realizing that to be the most effective, the average person should find a way to relate.

So, even if the source (the spirit teacher) may *seem* unreliable, it was only after those teachings were researched and made clear to me that I felt comfortable in sharing it in this book. And I believe that if you allow yourself to play with this material you'll find that it does make sense.

THE USE OF THE FOUR SYMBOL CARDS

The first step of this program begins with the practice of a visualization technique that has proven itself to be fun and very successful in classes and workshops over the last few years.

On the following pages you will find four symbol cards which will be your first link in beginning to see and recognize auras.

There is a history to the symbols; they can be traced to the most ancient of times. Their use provided connecting links to the mysterious cosmic powers of the universe and the powers' adaption to man, or vice versa.

They represent the four points of the compass and the four Archangels: Michael, Uriel, Raphael and Gabriel. Interestingly enough, these particular symbols can be found in the Tarot card deck representing each card in which they appear. With the Tarot card the Archangel is shown in picture or symbol form and the color associated with the card is also indicative of the Angel's power and purpose in educating man.

MICHAEL	▲	The North
URIEL	◡	The South
RAPHAEL	■	The East
GABRIEL	●	The West

These cards will help you develop your physical eyes to very subtle energy. The use of the cards will also help you associate the symbols with the colors.

The cards show you how aura colors and energies will look to you from the image that will linger on your eyes. This exercise only trains you by showing you what to expect; it does not reveal the aura.

INSTRUCTIONS

Use each symbol one at a time. After finding a empty/ blank, light colored surface such as a wall or ceiling, beginning with the triangle hold each card at eye-level and at arm's reach.

Stare into the symbol counting slowly from 1 to 15 and try not to blink. When you reach 15, remove the card quickly from your view and continue to stare straight ahead.

Almost instantly, you'll see the same shape floating in front of you in the place where the card was. This symbol will be different in color; it will be the opposite color of the card.

Continue to stare at the image until the shape disappears. Notice how soft the color and image are to your eyes. That's exactly how it will appear from the aura. After staring, your eyes may begin to water from holding the image. You will be exercising the optic nerve and training it to be more sensitive to higher vibrating energies. The more that you use these cards, the more skilled you will become.

Now, for some people, the image will take more time to appear and also some of the colors will appear easier than others. I know from my experience in the workshops that some people see the effect of one of the cards easier than that of another. My only thought as to the reason for this is that each person's vibrations are different. Therefore, each individual will see the color that's recognizable to that energy.

Of all the techniques I have encounted, these symbols and their usage are absolutely the very best way to open up and prepare one's self for viewing auras and the higher dimensions. After searching for years to find a way to teach how to see the aura, I was given this technique by a wonderful friend and confidant. Without using the symbols, it would take a much longer time to actually see the aura with your physical eyes.

It took me six months of experimenting and training to see a variety of color. You can achieve this in about one-third the time by using the symbol cards. Because the hardest thing to do when learning to see auras is to see color. Always the color easiest to see is the yellow-white glow surrounding someone's head. It really isn't color that you are seeing, it's just energy. This is how auras will appear to you until you can adapt yourself to seeing *true* color.

VISUALIZING

Everyone visualizes, though most would call it dreaming or day-dreaming. It's a time spent with the imagination dreaming of the perfect job, love, car, house, boat, clothing, or whatever. And when we love what we're dreaming about, we can see it clearly and get all of the feelings and sensations of being with it. It becomes a new and different reality for the time being or until we hold the vision and manifest it here in the physical world. You might be one of those people who dreamt of a new home and actually saw what it would look like. You envisioned the place before you got it. It was your future, waiting for you to catch up, AND YOU SAW IT. This happens with any idea or picture of something we desire. If we can really see it and feel it, we can have it. But it doesn't always happen as soon as we want it. If we hold to the belief no matter what and apply ourselves towards it, it will manifest.

Well, today most of us know about the sensational findings that have been connected with healing through visualization, so we know it's important. We also know it's important in goal achieving and making our life a happy and harmonious one.

This ability to see in different perspectives, using the mind's eye, can serve an even greater purpose. It can open a window allowing us to see into other dimensions. Through the use of visualization, we'll gear up our psyche and get it ready to begin to work with this inner vision.

When we talk about day-dreaming or imagination, many don't see the connection with visualization. If you have ever taken classes on awareness or meditation, you understand that most of us at one time or another had to strain to visualize something. It's as though we feel that we need to see a technicolor picture appearing right there in front of our eyes instantly in true, clear focus, and this isn't always the case. I think most of us try too hard to do something that's totally natural.

When we approach visualizing, we want to do it in fun. What sends you off on a journey into a day-dream? It's usually a pleasant feeling or thought. You allow yourself to slip easily into it. The same thing applies to visualization.

******

Here is an easy technique to begin your exercise. Simply relax with slow, easy breathing, close your eyes and look slightly up. This little step will activate the mind's eye.

******

Have you ever noticed that when you are asked a question, you usually look up and think before giving the answer? Funny, but true. It's a natural procedure. By doing this, the brain clicks into action and these instantaneous little pictures go flashing through your mind tracking down the information. The mind's eye is being put to everyday use.

What I have learned about visualization is this. I slowly let the feeling of the picture come to me. I let the feeling immerse me and off in the distance, barely peceptible, this little puzzle begins to form. I can hardly see it but I'm with the feeling, so I don't try to push it or speed up the process. I relax into the picture, loving the sensations I'm feeling. I let my heart lead me because the picture will come from any direction and can actually form itself off to the side instead of in front. I follow until the picture becomes clear and then I balance my sight with my feelings.

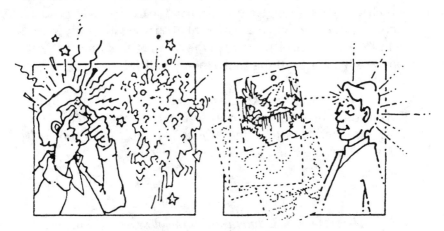

This shows a guy struggling to visualize.

This shows a happy visualizer feeling calm and relaxed and allowing the mind to create the picture at its own speed.

This same visualization process is involved with seeing auras. If you have a great interest in seeing them, you will, but you need to know a little about what an aura can look like in order to get the best concept of it. What makes up the aura? Is there more than one shape to an aura? These questions and more will be answered.

LEVELS OF THE AURA

As we sat in the group listening again to our Spirit Teacher, the Doctor, he asked us to observe the energy projecting from Diane's body. "Do you see the energy surrounding this body? Is it not like a bubble? Some would call it a cocoon. This bubble is the manifestation of many different movements, colors, and shapes resulting from the vibrations of any particular level of projection." (As you go along, what a projection is, will be made clear.)

Someone asked, "How many levels of projections are there?"

With a smile the Doctor acknowledged the question saying, "When you think, you are creating a vibration. This creation projects out from you. The same also happens when you express a feeling."

"All of your outer and inner expressions result in a manifestation of light vibration. We have a physical level, an emotional level, a mental level, and a level we can refer to as our inspirational level--the spiritual. So there are four basic levels. But there are many creations within each one."

"I know that you are anxious to see this phenomenon and you will. To help you open your 'eye', you should imagine that you are experiencing a bubble of light surrounding this body. You do not have to give this bubble a color, only imagine that it does exist. See it as a boundary, a soft line, that encircles the body at a distance. From your practice of imagining this bubble, you will begin to visualize what is truly there to see, but invisible to you now."

"Imagination and visualization are the keys to exercising the mind's eye. You then begin to train the physical eyes."

Let's discuss the four basic levels that make up the aura. Within each of the four levels are many others. Researchers studying the auric field have been concerned with the idea of healing. What the healers see is a cocoon filled with multiple bands (sometimes 50 and more) of lights and colors having many shades and hues with width in sizes and also depressions, thus leading to the idea of several levels.

There are some people who think there is only one aura and one level. Once we consider the basics of the energy and why it's there, we can easily understand the reason we have four.

We think, and when we do, we generate energy. And by the intensity we put into the thought, we project a burst of color that displays itself within the auric cocoon.

A good idea is expressed with a bright light.

The same holds true with our Emotions. When we're feeling good and on top of things, **we radiate**. People notice it. There's also that special glow of expectancy.

The Physical body creates its own level and presents other information besides health. It reveals our foundation in life, if we're grounded or not, and **the path we walk**, i.e., the direction we are taking ourselves and how we will be affected.

Encompassing the other three levels is the expansiveness of what and who we truly are. It's our Spiritual aura.

Explained on this page and shown in illustration on the following page are the levels and the order of their appearance from the body.

(1.) The Physical aura is the most dense in its energy and closest to the body. This energy remains with very little movement, a tightness in its appearance, expanding only a couple of feet. It looks like lots of little molecules grouped together.

(2.) The Emotional aura is next and this aura is felt and seen in waves flowing, spinning, and creating flashes. It's usually *the* easiest to come in contact with. The aura will flash around someone when he is telling a lie or being confronted with something he can't deal with. The energy jumps out a few feet and then retracts itself. The heart is connected with this level and will send its energy to another person over great distances if need be, or just across the room. Moody people can really be a problem to be around because they often want to project their moods on others. Anyone close to you in relationships, such as parents, children, working associates, or best friends, may want to dump on you with their emotions.

(3.) The Mental aura follows next and its energy is seen in geometrical shapes and forms that can be quite recognizable to the observing eye. If we look deeply enough into the aura, we can see these ideas in pictures appearing around the person.

(4.) The Spiritual aura is the highest vibrating level and the hardest to tune in. It's our protection. It's where the greatest records of our life are held and it won't reveal itself easily. Most people learning about aura reading will only get symbols here. This level is where Spirit Guides and past lives are seen and involves much time, effort, and patience to see.

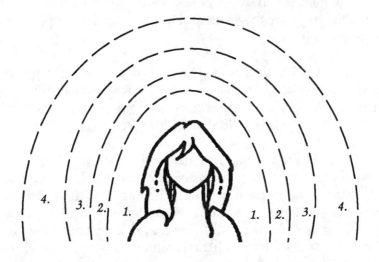

Aura levels

    This is how I first began to see the aura and after my third month in the group, I was able to distinguish the actual lines of difference between the aura levels.

HOW TO SEE THE AURA

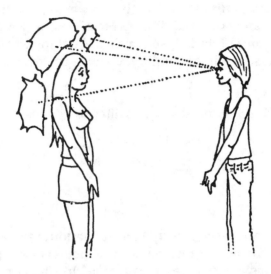

Yes. You truly can see the aura. And you will do this with your physical eyes while focusing your vision around the person in front of you.

Begin by finding a wall that is light in color and free from background disturbances. Have a friend stand in front of and a few feet away from the wall. The distance between the wall and your friend is important because you will want to have empty space to separate the aura energies from the third dimensional solid objects. You should then place yourself at least six feet away from him. Stare into the area above your friend's head and shoulders, as shown in the illustration. Try to take your friend out of focus while staring and concentrating on the aura.

It is a good idea to use the symbol cards to "warm-up" your vision before you begin. Allow your eyes to *relax* while applying a slight pressure from the back of your eyes, but don't hold a tight focus.

Again, while staring into the area above the head, begin to see the aura off in the corner of your mind, like the apple meditation, and persist until it becomes clear in your vision. Look in the area of the bubble which is about three to four feet from the person. Little by little, you will begin to see the colors appear.

Practice this exercise as often as you like.

****

It's been tremendously hard to introduce this ability to those who haven't yet discovered it within themselves. Most instructors have taken the easy way for lack of a better technique. The easy way is to close the eyes and focus in the direction of the body. Although this is the easiest way you will find better techniques as we proceed.

The closed eye technique is great for meditation in that it shuts out the world around you. It doesn't do a bit of good for seeing auras. Think about this. In my experiences, and some were quite 'hair-raising', if I had stopped to close my eyes to see the aura in front of me, I would have experienced a lot of problems. In everyday situations when I was choosing to go unnoticed with my ability, I wouldn't have been the effective person I was in a closed eye situation.

The closed eye techniques leave out a great deal of what there is to see.

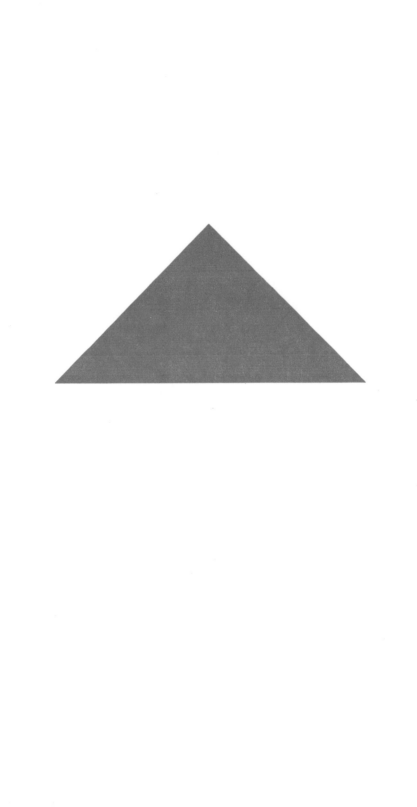

There is a bubble surrounding the body three to six feet in all directions: in front, in back, to the sides, above the head, and below. When looking at an aura, a person must look through his own aura first. It's a bubble, right? And it's in front of the person so, naturally it must be looked through.

SEEING YOUR OWN AURA

You can see your own by looking at a white wall or while in bed looking up at your ceiling. Take your eyes slightly out of focus and in a few moments you will notice little glimmers of light on the outside of your vision. These glimmers are yours and represent your aura. At times you might catch a glimpse of a bright light around you or a flash of color. It's not your eyes playing tricks, it's your aura.

Seeing your aura instead of the other person's aura will only happen at the beginning of the reading. When I look at an aura, I'm looking into a bubble that contains, to begin with, four levels of different vibrating energies. What happens? Don't the outer levels and colors cover up the inner ones? How is it that anyone can make heads or tails out of what level of energy he's picking up?

What I have done for you in this workbook is give you the benefit of my research and present a tool or graphic layout of a grid that will show you exactly what level you are tuning in.

The easiest areas to see within the area of the aura are the rounded places of the body, such as the head and shoulders, hands, elbows, knees, and feet. These areas give off the most radiance.

IS IT ETHICAL TO LOOK AT SOMEONE'S AURA?

This question comes up in the workshops. Seeing the basic aura of a person is no different than noticing the colors of the clothes he wears, his facial expressions, and his attitudes. All three things reveal something about the person.

When we look at just the basic colors of a person's aura, we're simply seeing his attitudes and feelings. If we cross the line and look deeper to see if we can read his mind or to try to find out a secret, we then make it unethical. This sort of practice or playing around will eventually come back to you, and you may not like it a bit. I never look into anyone's aura unless I'm invited.

THE FOUR STAGES OF AURA DEVELOPMENT

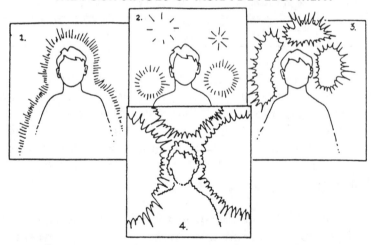

Beginning with step one, (notice the numbers on the illustrations) we expand our ability to see more. The magnetic body is first. This body projects earth magnetic energies to the densest aura degree. This body is the result of what is seen in Kirlian photography. The rest of what you will see are the aura levels discussed earlier. The more we work at allowing ourselves to envision the aura the better we will be.

```
┌ ─ ─ ─ ─ ─ ─ ─ ─ ─ ─ ─ ─ ─ ─ ─ ─ ┐
          SECTION TWO
  COLORS and the COLORING EXERCISE
└ ─ ─ ─ ─ ─ ─ ─ ─ ─ ─ ─ ─ ─ ─ ─ ─ ┘
```

NOTHING IS REALLY SOLID

BASIC COLORS OF THE COLOR WHEEL

EARTH COLORS

ADDITIONAL COLORS

COLORING EXERCISES

COLORS

The atomic structure of the physical universe begins with energy particles. The particles vibrate creating light and sound in accordance to their speed. How fast they vibrate makes the colors that we see. The ranges of light available for us are contained within a spectrum. The spectrum has been divided into its basic form with the invention of the color wheel. Our concentration will be focused on the primary and secondary colors.

" *Nothing is really solid.*"

Because our bodies are structured with atomic particles, it should be easy to assume that we vibrate light. Like a light bulb with a shade covering it, our internal light is softened through the body. Nothing is really solid. Atoms and molecules are individual entities spinning around on a field of energy and not touching. There is space between them. This space allows intake of light from a much higher, more subtle vibrational dimension.

This pure light energy is slowed down, condensed, and adapted to travel at the speed required to function in the physical reality. It is processed through our subconscious and into our daily lives, feeding us with the energy we need to function.

How we function with the Light is up to us. If we live harmonious lives (living true to who we are) then the energy flows and we receive pure Light energy in return. Remember: The key is living true to who *we* are, our individual path. *That* insures our energy intake. Whether our function looks good or bad to others is of no consequence to our intake. THIS IS A UNIVERSAL LAW.

A question is asked, "Which colors are good and which ones are bad?"

We answer that, "There really are no bad colors. In their pure state all colors are good and useful. When light is blocked or slowed down it will loose its effectiveness and become gray or dull. A bad thought or feeling can cause this by creating disorder in the intake and flow. By not moving in a harmonious state of being, we throw off or block the intake of the energy and create '*bad*' colors, like when someone remarks on the dark cloud over another's head. The person who is receiving the bad remark is 'out-of-sorts' with himself, troubled, angry, or depressed."

Another question is asked, "How many colors are there in the aura?"

We answer with, "Everyone has at least seven colors appearing in the aura with a variety of shades and hues. The colors can range from solid to translucent, and pastel to dense.

The last question is, "Do colors change?"

We finish by answering, "The colors of the aura will expand or shrink in their area, but no, they won't really change. The only time colors change within the aura is after a change in lifestyle is made which is usually a *major* change."

The following descriptions of color are held to be universal. If mathematics can prove the existence of matter then we can assume that energy vibrating at a specific speed can affect other matter and its surroundings by the speed of its light particles. This is to say that Red creates an effect on other energy, but can only do what Red does, and cannot assume the duties of another color with the same effect. The same is true for all colors. Each color has its own use.

> At the beginning of each color description you'll find a list of simple meanings of the color interpretation. This list will be referred to on occasion.

COLOR DESCRIPTIONS

RED ... the densest color on the wheel. Red creates the most friction. This friction attracts our attention. We are making a statement when we use and create with this color. The emotions created by red can range from the fire of raging passion and anger to the soft warmth of love and affection. It shows us STOP and EXIT signs as well. The mid-point of this vibration is good, clear, "go-get-'em", goal achieving energy. Red that has a dark gray or muddy look, such as crimson, shows anger and perhaps some hatred in there, too. You'll also "feel" the energy coming from the person who is projecting red.

A nice pure red is the color of attraction. When you wish to attract attention to yourself, you wear it. When I see this color appearing in someone's aura, most of the time, it tells of a goal, and it usually doesn't take up much area in the aura. It backs up an idea to move the idea forward or generates attraction for it. Red is a very useful color, as all colors are. There is such a good, warm feeling wrapped up in a true color like Red. Think of Christmas and Valentine's Day.

ORANGE ... the color of vitality, vigor, good health, and sexual excitement. Wherever this is spotted in the aura, you can pretty much choose from the above. A burnt orange can show tiredness. The burnt area is usually around the fringes of a dull orange.

Have you noticed how much orange is now being used to attract attention? All of the 'Safety' cones and signs and the jackets worn by highway workers are good examples of this. It seems the vibrations for all of us are raising and we're becoming attracted to higher colors. The fast food chains, banks, and department stores are using oranges to decorate their interiors so that their customers feel in an "up-beat" mood.

YELLOW ... The color of awakening ... the morning sun ... the birth of creativity and inspiration. It includes the use of intelligent action or intelligence shared. It's the light bulb above the cartoon character's head.

Every teacher has it. Every artist, performer, and smart businessman will also have a good yellow above his head. Yellow shows creativity at work or a readiness to be creative.

GREEN ... what a comfortable color. When nature thrives, it resonates this. It's the color of health, growth, balance, and change. This also happens to be the cycles of Mother Nature. Health leads to growth that leads to balance that leads to change. Again choose from the above list when green appears in the aura. An emerald green shows completeness of an endeavor and it can be considered the color of a good teacher. Why? Because its knowledge is earned.

BLUE ... a very pleasant color. Blue can be cool, calm, collected. It works well with communication because the energy flows like water. It can represent peace and spirituality.

Blue provides sensitivity and yet it can make the best of barriers against warmer energies. The old proverbial 'cold shoulder' treatment is the best way to describe what blue can do.

PURPLE ... the most sensitive color on the wheel. Purple provides a combination of wisdom and understanding. When seen within the aura, Purple can show how sensitive someone is being about a situation. Purple has the ability to move *into* the other colors and bring out the information connected with it. The true psychics radiate this color from their auras. In the future, if you don't see this color in use and you are getting psychic advice, be very discriminating about the information and the source.

Royalty and Religious Leaders have worn this color exclusively for centuries and they have been known for their wisdom and understanding on most occasions.

As the vibrations of the planet are rising, so is our consciousness, people are becoming more curious about their own psychic ability. Naturally, purple is a popular color today.

EARTH COLORS

There are more colors that you'll come across as you explore the aura. These colors are of the earth, the colors of nature: browns, tans, rust-red, colors of the seasons, forest greens, wildflowers, ocean blue, turquoise, harvest gold.

There are masculine and feminine colors. These colors reflect the energies of those who live and work in that kind of environment. Those who work outside and with the earth or those who know they can benefit by the grounding effect these energies supply can utilize these colors. The more earth colors we have in our aura, the more we connect with earth energies. And being connected with the earth is not always limiting. (Some of you might have considered earth energy colors to be limiting as far as taking away from spirituality.) But earth energies can be very nurturing to the self and the growth process.

SOME ADDITIONAL COLORS

PEACH ... This color shows generosity. It is a mixture of red, orange, and yellow.

LAVENDER ... This color vibration is very high. By seeing a translucent lavender, and to me it looks like an amethyst, you are tuning in to a Master Teacher's energy. This color of energy can be used to raise the consciousness/vibrations of the energy around it. Lavender transmutes other energy to its vibration. Lavender is associated with the feminine principal, while the next color, gold, is associated with the masculine principal.

SILVER ... reveals an awakening of consciousness to the Universe and its Laws. It also shows abundance and money.

GOLD ... the most sought-after energy. This is the color of the Higher Self. With the right use of this energy, we can be protected from negativity. Gold is the other Master Teacher vibration that can transmute light. It's very attractive to others and can provide great healings and wonderful outcomes to problems and goals.

The higher vibrational colors (lavender, deep violet, gold, and translucents) can be used to raise the consciousness of you and others. Try feeling the difference of colors in meditation. *Pastels feel soft*. More light than usual is being projected into the basic color thereby creating the softness. Muddy colors feel heavy.

WHITE ... reflects other colors. This *can* create aloofness and separative energies because it keeps out other colors. But it can also be used as protection.

BLACK ... consumes other colors/light. It draws light to itself. Wearing the energy of black hides your feelings from others and creates privacy.

** Wearing white or black is fine as long as you mix other colors with them.**

By the way, you wear the colors that fit your aura. Ever notice how you change clothes several times on occasion before going somewhere? And how some colors don't 'feel' right? They need to fit your vibration of the moment for you to feel comfortable. Bright colors don't feel good for depression or sickness.

COLORING EXERCISE

I am going to introduce you to an idea that was passed on to me by a friend when I first began working in Los Angeles as a psychic in 1980 at a Psychic Fair which employed about twenty-five psychics. This was the first time for me to "read" in the public instead of at home. There was lots of competition. And I mean just that. Many of those working were not really coming from a spiritual space and seemed to be more concerned with the cash and future clients. They high-powered their psychic abilities using lots of pizazz and good gimmicks. Well, I had to learn to swim or sink. I wanted to develop my talent and I decided that the best way to do it was to join in with the energy and go with it.

People who attended psychic fairs usually understood that most psychics use Tarot Cards, Crystal Balls, Palmistry, or Astrology as tools for fortune telling. Very few had heard about aura reading. So, initially, I had problems generating interest.

I began making friends with a few of the other psychics, but generated few readings. Understanding my dilemma, a fellow worker mentioned an aura reader she had recently gone to see for a reading, away from the fair. She said the aura reader drew a sketch of the client's aura and suggested that I try the same method. It didn't take much time to realize that this was probably the idea I needed to generate a better response.

I drew a chart with a figure of a body and put four encircling lines around it representing the four levels of the aura. I made 50 charts and took them to the fair along with a box of 48 pastels. My work picked up using the charts and a great deal of new information emerged about the aura.

The two rooms the fair was held in were not big compared to the amount of psychics that had to use them. We were bunched in side by side using coffee tables with only wooden dividers to separate my client and me from another psychic and his client. The middle of the room, which wasn't all that wide, was lined with chairs that were back-to-back for potential customers to sit and wait. Most of the time the room was packed with people, so it left very little privacy. Everytime I would begin to tune in to a client's aura by looking around him, someone walking by would stick his face into the area I was looking into. Well, that was really difficult to deal with.

Tuning in an aura is the same as tuning in a radio station. In an area where there are lots of stations, like a city, even the slightest movement of the dial changes the station you are listening to and sometimes driving a couple of blocks can take you out of the reception area. When I sat in the room and tried to zero in on a client, any passing aura frequency would interrupt my ability to have a clear reception.

Well, this is where my learning took off. There were only ten to twelve minutes allotted to each reading and if I wanted to be good, it meant I had to be fast in getting the information out. I couldn't spend time fumbling around. I would introduce myself, find out their name, explain a little of what I was going to do and then look at their aura for a few seconds.

As soon as I 'locked' into a color, I immediately took the color from the pastel box and colored it on the chart in the same place that I saw it in the aura. As I did more of these drawings, a familiar inner switch would turn on as soon as I got my first impression of the aura. I no longer needed to look up at my client until the drawing was done. My inner feelings would see the colors and direct me to the area on the chart where it belonged. When I was finished, I would explain what the colors meant.

There was one good lesson I learned when I first began. Sometimes I would get a person who had lots of dark blue in his aura. At the time I really had no idea what it meant. I would say something to him about what I was picking up but he couldn't relate to it. After I said five or six things, it became apparent that I wasn't tuning in, so I would return his ticket. I struggled with this through about ten people until the answer came to me. Since I hadn't experienced the problem before, this was totally new to me.

Reading at Psychic Fairs is a lot different than reading in private where you have more time to spend with each person. Working at Fairs, you have to jump right in. The dark blue was a barrier to keep me out. Subconsciously, these people didn't want to show me their auras. The blue was cold and kept me out. I was getting "The Cold Shoulder." Whenever someone intentionally blocks me from seeing his aura I will either get nonsense from my perceptions or simply see things that belong to myself.

See what I'm saying about all the different kinds of information inside an aura? It's very hard to get right to the point of someone's creation and to see the true reality of what's taking place without his complete cooperation.

Allow me to backtrack here a moment. The lessons with the Doctor in Santa Cruz covered basics concerning aura energies and chakras, energy exchanges, and healing. Since healing was not my chosen field and psychic reading is, I received very little training for that. I was left to my own resources to find out what I needed to know. My only ideas came from my readings with a Clairvoyant. I had watched how he looked around me to see things, so that was my only clue as to how to read an aura. I employed the basics I learned from the Doctor and the Clairvoyant and went from there. So although I had spent five years looking at auras, these had been learning years without a psychic mentor to instruct me in the ways of reading correctly. I met that mentor, Jim Watson, at the fair, but we didn't get together until the following year.

If you are simply out to have fun and to satisfy your curiosity about auras, you'll do it with no problem. To see a few colors around a person doesn't take all that much to accomplish. But to read someone accurately requires practice, a good overall knowledge of people, and knowledge of yourself and your ability.

****

The following pages will take you through the technique of coloring and provide "already completed" readings. I'll guide you through three readings, step by step.

ABOUT THE COLORING

Let's talk about coloring and why I feel it's beneficial for you. As you will see later on in this book, there will be a certain pattern that will lay itself out for you. This pattern is the result of catching the energy in a 'freeze frame', like one frame of a moving picture. Thoughts and emotions can continuously change during the course of the reading. By catching the energy in a coloring, we can get right to the true picture and no matter what is introduced into the aura from that point, we can work from the first impressions.

The following exercise will help you become familiar with coloring the aura. By now, you should have in your possession some pastels or crayons. I supply the workshop participants with a box of 24 crayons, so they have a good selection to choose from.

As you practice on your own with these exercises, on the first few drawings you will feel like you're making up the impressions that you receive. In the workshops, participants draw these charts five or six times. With each chart, we get a different volunteer to stand in front of the group. I like to alternate between sexes so we can see the difference. The people look over the volunteer for about ten seconds and then look down at the chart and begin to grab from the crayons the colors that attract *their* attention and place them where *they think* they should go. We do this exercise as fast as possible so no one feels like they are borrowing ideas from someone sitting next to them. Most of them will get three colors that are the same and some will even have them in the same area. This is a very convincing exercise. It lets them see that they really are picking up on the aura through their feelings. Interestingly, those doing this exercise have gotten 60% to 80% overall accuracy dealing with the volunteer's current life on their first few tries.

I've given the names John and Mary to the two figures appearing on three charts. Surrounding both of them on the charts are patterns/shapes that are numbered. Each number corresponds to a color. The color will tell us something about the person, such as how he is thinking, feeling, and expressing himself.

Each color and shape is explained with an interpretation in a list preceding the chart. The first chart appears on page 41. Go by the numbers and color in the shapes. Read about its meaning first, and then color. This will help you make the connection between the conscious mind and the psychic self.

****

Follow along ..... here is your first example reading.

Our first chart is Mary. She's just come to me for a reading. After a brief introduction, (it's better to know as little as possible about the person so there are no preconceptions about what I'll tune-in), I have a chart in front of me and my colors are easily accessible. I study the aura for just a few seconds telling myself to tune in, while I look over as much of the aura as is possible to see—head to toe. As soon as I perceive a color from the aura, I begin.

When I color I'm not trying to do a pretty picture or masterpiece. I scribble in the color wherever it feels appropriate. Now sometimes I feel like pressing the color hard and sometimes softly which shows the intensity of the energy. Usually I won't look back up too soon. As I apply one color, the area for that color may expand to multiple locations while a new color is springing into my mind.

I normally get two or three different impressions connected to the first. I do my best at never second-guessing the color that my hand is directed to, because the color is usually the correct one. Now sometimes the shade of color may be different than the one in my hand, so I trade it.

I show Mary the chart and begin to tell her about the colors and what they mean. I look into the aura for the impression connected to the color. (The impression may consist of either sight or feel.) This is done until all the colors have been explained.

COLOR LIST FOR MARY'S CHART

1.) *YELLOW.*   It's a very clear, soft but radiant, color--close around the head and torso area. Yellow says that Mary is very creative and she's sending out some very positive vibrations. The Yellow at her left hand means she's reaching into the future to attract more.

2.) *ROSE.*   A soft red or pink color resting beside the yellow reveals a warm sensitivity with the emotions. This color reveals that Mary is very attractive and pleasant to be around.

(3.) *GREEN.*   Green resting above the head and leaning toward the past shows changes are occuring with her. My insight tells me that she has recently begun bringing things into balance with her thinking. This balance moves her closer to her goals as seen with the color flowing from her left foot. The green flowing from her right hand designates the timing as to when the event began. Notice how far away from her body the color reaches. That's the starting point.

(4.) *LIGHT-BLUE.*   This color seeks clarity for right decision making and mixing spiritual and mental energies as it positions itself above the head in the area of the past. It again appears near the knee and foot of the same side of the body. This promotes a good and proper foundation.

(5.) *MEDIUM BROWN.*   Mary was being too "down-to-earth" in the past. She limited herself with her thoughts. She was being a real "stick-in-the-mud."

(6.) *PURPLE.*   Mary is tuning in to her spiritual self at the present. She's receiving inner guidance and being open to it. This is a lesson about the new cycle she is entering. The purple tells me that she will gain, or has the opportunity to gain, wisdom from the up-coming months. The purple appearing in the future at the level of her everyday life.

(7.) *ORANGE.*   This is a very positive addition to her future energies. The orange will provide vitality in the higher mental levels of her aura, allowing her to easily move through stubborn areas that might appear along the way. It supplies confidence.

Overall, Mary's aura is in good shape. She has successfully moved through a stagnant phase in her life and is in the process of creating some very enthusiastic energy that will back her intuitive powers for direction in the coming six months.

When I talk to Mary, we discuss timing. This is something you probably questioned as you read it from the list of meanings. There are two charts following these three on readings that will illustrate the different areas such as timing and day-to-day happenings.

Another procedure with the aura readings goes like this: While talking to Mary and discussing the colors on the chart, I look at the aura to confirm the colors.

<u>This could take some time, but look at your chart and envision the same color pattern in the area of the aura that you have on the paper.</u> This really helps develop your sight because intuitively you've already seen it and now you want your physical eyes to pick it up. <u>You want to begin seeing the aura in the same way you colored it on the paper.</u> Use this back and forth method while giving the reading.

If I've gone into the reading a ways and need to cover another area, the chart reminds me of what I saw earlier and then I can move right into it.

COLOR LIST OF JOHN'S READING

One of the first things you'll notice about John's aura is the different structure of the shapes compared to Mary's. Consider the average differences between men and women. Men use the thinking, logical side of themselves while women work with their intuitiveness. Intuituion is emotional energy; the logical is the mind. Normally you will find the energies between the sexes like this, even though both can have similar vibrations.

1. *BROWN.* These are mixtures of different shades of brown. These colors provide the foundation and create grounded-ness to get things accomplished in the physical.

2. *YELLOW.* John is in a creative mood as the color is good and clear. Until all is tied together in the reading, the yellow is only expressing ideas and creativity. After working on the reading, it is seen as a presently good idea that will manifest in the future according to the two areas in his future: one on the mental and the other on the day-to-day level.

③ *ORANGE.*   Orange is an energetic color that's spinning around the physical body.

④ *RED.*   This is a good clear red used to attract the goals he wants to accomplish. We see the red in certain areas but feel it's projecting throughout his entire aura.

⑤ *GREEN.*   This color looks fluorescent because it's the physical stability and health. The green in the future is softer and relates to good emotional balance.

⑥ *BLUE.*   Medium light blue is the color here which is good and clear. This color creates clarity and is expressing itself as it projects from above his head to down around the shoulders.

⑦ *SILVER.*   Because of the position of the silver in the inspiration level, John has a good chance of getting on track with his finances. It appears that more money could be in his future through advancement of work in probably about five or six months from now.

⑧ *DARK GREEN.*   John is struggling.

⑨ *MUDDY BLUE-GREEN.*   Within the last four months, John moved through a very frustrating and limiting period, a real bummer of a time. But now things are better.

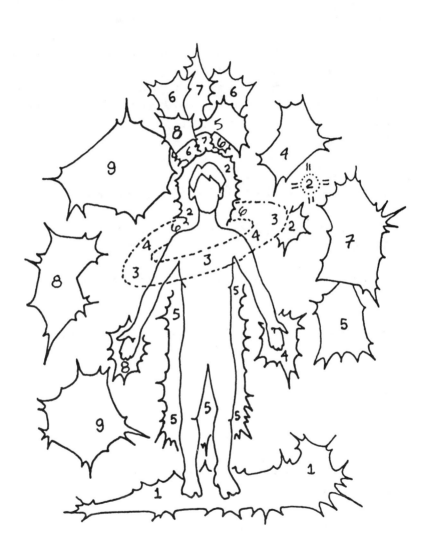

We have looked at two "good charts" and I think it would also be of value to see a "lousy" one. This example can be for either sex.

When I look at the person, I first recognize how heavy his energy is and how muddy the tone is. This fellow has some heavy problems that he may or may not be dealing with. When I talk with him, I work at being as easy going as possible while confirming his problems and I try to see where he may be able to help himself.

COLOR LIST FOR A PROBLEM AURA

All colors connected with this drawing will have a muddy or dark gray tone.

(1.) *GREEN.*   This color shows confusion and an out-of-balance situation with his energies.

(2.) *DARK BLUE.*   He is unclear and unsure about things.

(3.) *BROWN.*   This color indicates he is overly stuck.

(4.) *YELLOW.*   Ideas and creativity are at a real low; he has no inspiration. In the past, the furthest shape to his right, the Yellow is good, but then it begins to fade to Gray as it gets closer to the Green showing the beginning of the problem.   But close to his head, the color is brighter because it refects the present and he's working at being a little more cheerful. The Yellow in the future surrounded by Orange is a better yellow than the other two, clearer and brighter.

(5.) ORANGE.   The energy he wants to apply to free him from feeling so stagnate about his future.

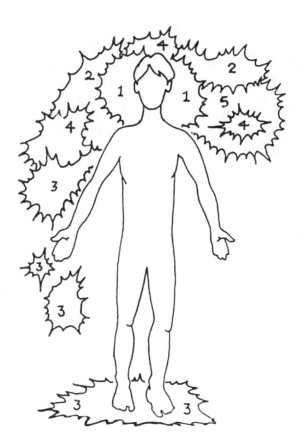

TWO ILLUSTRATIONS OF THE AURA LEVELS
AND
THE INTERPRETATION OF THE AREA

      This section will name the levels that were talked about in the reading. The illustrations are all part of the whole. They will be seen separately or together depending on your choice and ability to see. By knowing the levels and their placement in the aura, you'll intermix these levels when you want. The improvement in using your aura-sight will leave little doubt as to the accuracy of this information.

Description of chart #1.

      After becoming aware of the different levels of the aura contained within a bubble, you will begin to see the aura as in the coloring. This diagram more or less formed itself after I spent many years of research. The more I read for people concerning their lives, the more the aura displayed itself to me in this chart which reveals an abundance of information. Timing appears in the aura and can be detailed in the chart. Also, the chart allows the information to be divided among mental, emotional, physical, inspirational, and everyday reality. This diagram shows how one level may affect another.

CHART #1

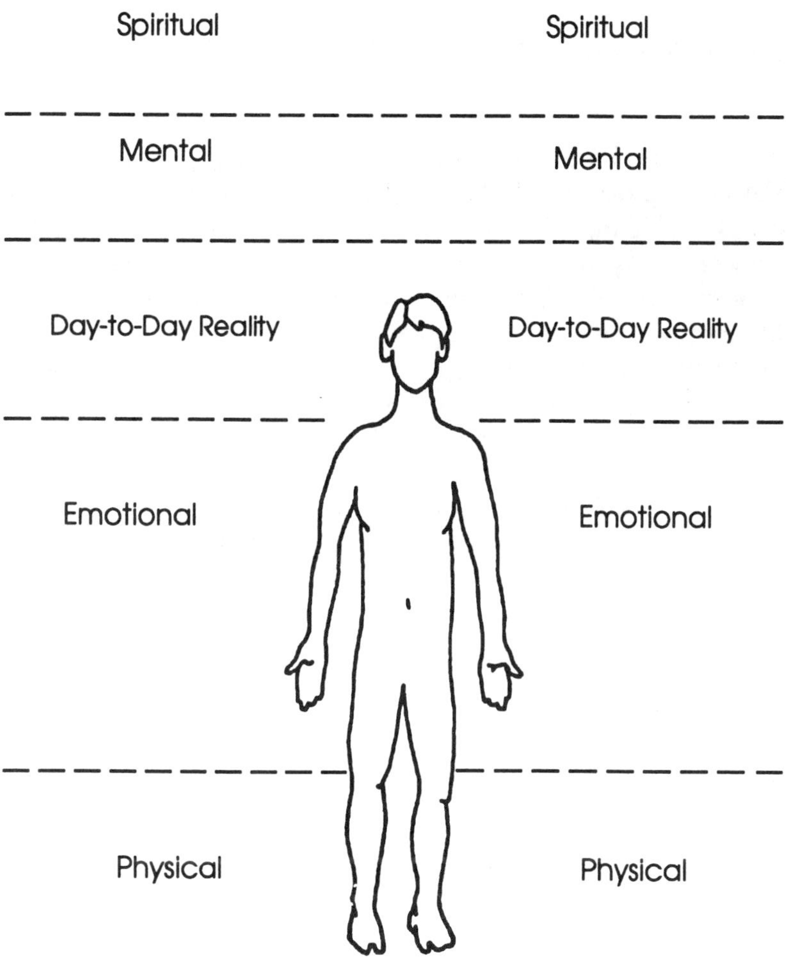

Spiritual	Spiritual
Mental	Mental
Day-to-Day Reality	Day-to-Day Reality
Emotional	Emotional
Physical	Physical

Description of chart #2.

This chart deals with timing. Although timing can be
flexible in a reading, and it usually is, this diagram can provide
a good guideline. The magnetic energy of the planet controls the
flow of energy by which we live. Above the equator to the north,
all energy circulates from the left to right. South of the equator,
the energy circulates from right to left. Those of us in the northern
hemisphere receive energy from our left as it passes through us
in a clockwise flow then leaves our aura to the right. So the future
is seen to the left, the present is above and closely surrounding
the body, and the past is to the right. Most of our cycles of creation
for our goals and desires shift every six months. If I want to bring
something important to myself, many times I concentrate on this
for at least six months from the point of getting the idea or
inspiration, to actually seeing some kind of results. So, my
overall timing evolves from six months to a year with each
reading in either direction, past or future.

Notice that there are three zones for timing surrounding
the body. These zones can be flexible. The diagram gives you an
approximate time so that your inner self can tell you what timing
it is picking up.

CHART #2

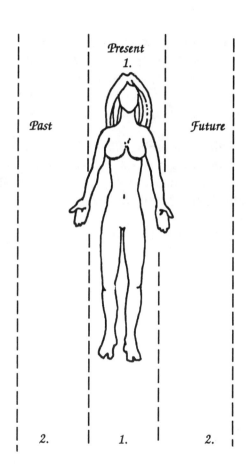

1. Present Time
2. Two weeks to Four months
3. Six months and further

COLORING THE AURA
WHILE LOOKING AT YOUR SUBJECT

We have now reached a point in the exercises when we progress another step. This part of the workshop takes place after the participants have practiced a few colorings of the aura without looking at the subject. With the awareness of using the feeling senses just gained, we now look and feel at the same time.

Following the earlier illustration of viewing the aura, have your friend again stand in front of you against a light background. Stare into the area around your friend and color on the chart whatever you can feel and see.

It is important to immediately color your perceptions of your friend's energy. By failing to do this you may miss an image that may prove to be important to the coloring and reading. The mistake of not immediately marking the chart happens by getting caught up in wanting to see too many things in the beginning. Please allow yourself the benefit of taking your time to catch everything possible.

It is also a good idea not to spend more than 3-5 minutes coloring your chart. Too much time spent at first, may create confusion in your *receptions* and basically wear you out.

I always include the body with my coloring, looking for blockages of energy from head to toe and at the chakra points that will be explained later on. In the worksheet section at the back of this book you will find pictures of male and female bodies that you may use for your practice in coloring.

SECTION THREE
ASTRAL LIGHTS and SPINNING WHEELS

THE PSYCHIC SELF

VIEWING ASTRAL ENERGIES

CHAKRAS

SPIRIT GUIDES

ASTRAL LIGHTS AND SPINNING WHEELS

This is a fun name for this section of the book and describes what we will be discovering, talking about, and then using.

Imagination is the key to experiencing auras. Imagination and the psychic self are strongly linked. Imagination provides freedom for this inner self to explore new avenues away from the normal mundane activities of each day.

THE PSYCHIC SELF

The Psychic Self can be thought of as a child. And like a child, it wants encouragement to work with us to help fulfill those desires we have. We tend to yell at ourselves on occasions when we screw up and our Psychic Self thinks we are yelling at him, so he doesn't like telling us too much. Think about those times when you wanted to do something and a voice inside you told you not to do it and you went ahead and did it anyway. You said to yourself, "I knew I shouldn't have done that," or "I knew that would happen." Well, everytime you got upset for not listening to that inner voice, you were turning away from your Psychic Self and each time you did, that part of you decided to become more detached from your conscious mind. It didn't want to disturb you so it sent the information to the back of your mind.

We choose our focus when we are in contact with another. And many times we are blind to the reality of what's going on. And that goes both ways. Someone could really be sending out "hello, I love you" vibrations and we could be in a funk about our confidence and totally miss the boat if we are looking for rejection instead of acceptance.

It's important for us to communicate with our Psychic Self as often as possible if we want to bring contact with it to a prominent place in our everyday lives. All the true psychics I know, ones who are in the business of counseling and teaching others, use their ability everyday and practice communicating with themselves in a variety of ways. They play little games by asking questions like, "Who's telephoning me right now?" when the phone rings, or "I wonder what's in the mail today?" when they go to their mail box, or "Who's thinking of me right now?" This is how they train themselves and become better at their trade.

The easiest way to open the channel to our Psychic Self is to play games just like the psychics. Playing games isn't threatening to our ego and it shouldn't be. That's why imagination is important. It's like playing a 'make-believe' game. If we relax and play a game with seeing and feeling the aura, our Psychic Self plays right along with us and lets all kinds of stuff come through.

Now that I've spoken of this self of our's, let's become more familiar with it. Whenever I get information that's helpful from my inner voice, I thank it out loud by saying, "Thanks Psychic Self!" and I pat myself on the back. I've learned that the more I thank that part of me and do it out loud, the more it responds to my needs. Be spontaneous; go with your simplest feelings about a situation. If you're lost while driving, get relaxed. By slowing down your mind and asking quietly for directions you'll help yourself in the best way possible. Your feelings will guide you to the best possible end, whether it's the right road to turn down or the right person to get directions from. Trust in your inner self and you'll recognize your own psychic powers.

VIEWING ASTRAL ENERGIES

The more we gain with our ability, the more we will see from the aura. In the beginning we will encounter subtle lighting, shadowy effects, and some movement. Although we may find this limiting, it is still enough to recognize that we are seeing the aura. We are adapting our inner and outer eyesight together with our feeling nature, one step at a time.

My work with auras may be different than what has been written or discussed in other material by other authors. I have chosen not to work with healing the physical body, so how I see and work with auras is different. We will now begin to learn how to 'psychically' read auras by tuning in to the **ASTRAL ENERGIES** .

Most of us usually concentrate on a few things at a time and these will be expressed as the most noticeable energies in our aura. Such as our work, relationships, money, goals, etc. These expressions will be seen close to the body and around the head. For me, when I look at someone's aura whatever appears first to my attention is their focus.

Once we have a good bond with our psychic self we can let it know what kind of expressions we would like to see from auras, such as, persons attracted to us, thoughts or feelings directed towards us, welcome signs or go away signs, anything that can be beneficial to us. Our goal should be to work with that self to manifest a better life.

As we go forward with these exercises we will be looking for earthly reactions from the aura and not just health or personality colors.

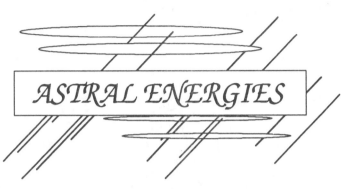

are the result of the sub-levels to the standard energy vibrational frequencies we have been discussing. If we were to jog a little to the side of the frequencies that we are normally functioning in, we would encounter the astral.

* * * * * * *

Let's imagine concentrating on the physical level of the aura and as we do we look a little differently at it by accessing the astral. Usually the physical aura would show us health or vitality levels, but by accessing the astral we can now see the directions the body is traveling and the responses it will encounter in that movement.

Follow along with the four illustrated examples of everyday (astral energy) auras.

1.) John's aura is **Bright Green** and is saying that he's in good health and that he is demonstrating balance in his affairs.

2.) Mary is in the middle of some very good thoughts. A **Bright Yellow** shines in the two shapes closer to the shoulders. The center shape is White and is receiving Clear Light from above.

3. Here, John is having a creative idea concerning his business. Floating around his head are **Clear Silver** pointed shapes. A charged-up **Blue** beams from his shoulders suggesting that he can 'feel' his inspiration.

4. Mary can be a little shy at times. The three larger shapes are **Soft Blue** and they feel like they're being held closely to her body. The two smaller shapes are **Soft Pink** which shows her gentle and attractive nature.

CHAKRAS

The name Chakra comes from an East Indian word for wheel. Chakras are energy centers within us and when activated spin like wheels. Each Chakra projects a flow of vibrating energy through it that creates a color and sound corresponding to its location in the body.

Within the physical body resides a body double, a spiritual body. This is the body that holds the Chakras. Think of this body as a prism, and from above light is projected downward and received and then passed on slowing down the speed and solidifying the substance—to the physical. The physical body uses this energy for life sustainment. You need this "Spiritual Light" to live just as you need air and water. It's the Life Force of the Universe. This light then refracts through the Chakras, which are set up to utilize it to their own natural make up, and like the facets of a prism they create the colors of the rainbow, or the light spectrum.

They may resemble a flower, in the sense that when it (the Chakra) is closed, it will look like a young bud that hasn't opened. And when open, looks like a flower in bloom. **A spinning wheel of light and color** that flows out and away from the center, only to move back into itself from beneath, turning itself inside out over and again. They are very beautiful to gaze upon when "in bloom."

Because they belong to the spiritual body, they can and will rotate in a 360 degree radius, projecting light from the front, back, and to each side when consciously used for that purpose.

There are nine main Chakras. Seven (7) within the body proper and two (2) above the head. Each one operates by how well we are doing in each particular area of expression.

The question is asked, "What purpose can the chakras serve when interpreting an aura?"

My answer to this is, "When I first started seeing auras in our group meetings the purpose or goal was spiritual enlightenment. By seeing the Chakras, we could see how much light was projecting from our friend's body and judge its quality by the clearness of the color. The quality denoted how clear the person was becoming in the advancement of self. We would speak of our perceptions in that manner."

"Once I began reading the aura for psychic fairs, the way I viewed the Chakras became different. This time they spoke of situations and how the energy (the person) was flowing in them. So each color spoke of something and each chakra had its own color, thereby giving a specific quality of action and response to each center."

"Let's say there is a problem in communication between you and a friend, and you don't want to talk it out even though you know you should. Your Throat Chakra would react to this and show the energy being blocked by clouding the color and closing the center part way. If indeed you were to talk things over and express yourself like you know you should, then the energy would flow again and the color would be much clearer."

"To finish my answer, I now see the Chakra at the mundane level, a level that expresses more of the everyday life than the Spiritual Being. This helps me tune in to people at a place that's important to most."

****

Well, it's all interrelated anyway. You'll see from the Chakras what you choose to see, at the level (physical, emotional, mental, or spiritual) you choose. This is the basic teaching of the program. Your Higher Mind will select the way in which you utilize your ability and reveal it to you in sight and feel. This may mean that you will only tune in to the healing aspect of working with this knowledge and not any psychic work or vice-versa.

The illustration provided shows the chakras and lists them by the density of their light vibrations, (1 through 9), with the number one being the densest. Below you will find a list describing each Chakra and how it represents its energy flow.

(1.) The *"POWER CHAKRA"* ... resides at the base of the spine and is connected to the reproductive glands. The color is **RED**. This center represents not only sex but also survival and can be very animalistic. This area can also pertain to Goal Seeking with aggressive or assertive movement.

(2.) The *"ENERGY CHAKRA"* ... sitting in the lower stomach area shows the body's vitality and health. East Indian thought connects it with sexual energy. The color is **ORANGE**.

(3.) The *"CREATIVE CHAKRA"* ... The stomach is the spot where we do our heaviest thinking. Ever notice how worry can cause an upset stomach? Even though it's ironic, that is the down-side to this Chakra. The color is **YELLOW**. This center's dynamics gives us Thoughts, Ideas, and Will Power.

(4.) The *"HEART CHAKRA"* ... rests over the heart and with it we feel and seek to understand. With understanding, we seek to unify and balance our lives with those around us. Love is the beauty of this Chakra. The color is **GREEN**. Of course, its negatives include vanity, jealousy, and envy.

(5.) The *"THROAT CHAKRA"* ... sits right around the area of the "Adam's Apple." Its purpose is communication: how we are speaking, if we are, and how it is being received by our environment and the people around us. Its color is **BLUE**.

(6.) The "INNER-EYE CHAKRA" ... is above and in-between our eyes. The pictures of dreams, imaginings, and insight come from this center. It's how we are viewing the world around us. When the color is regulating itself through an awakening consciousness, it will vibrate the light of Violet. Normally this Chakra is supposed to be **INDIGO** ... with violet next in the Chakra line. But as we begin to open this center, the veil of Indigo is lifted (the vibrations are sped up) into Violet. We were taught that by working with the new color, our awakening would take on a quicker pace to realization. So this color should be **VIOLET**.

(7.) The "CROWN CHAKRA" ... sits at the top of the head but in an area that allows for the in-coming energy to flow down the spine. This color is really no color but **CLEAR** ... **WHITE**. If we are to imagine light flowing into the body it is most helpful to envision it as clear, so that as it descends the spine and then up the front through the Chakras it can adapt itself to each without interference or changing its quality.

(8.) The "COSMIC CHAKRA" ...Rarely mentioned, this Chakra is our link to Universal Thought. It introduces awareness and higher knowledge at the beginning level. It speaks to us with the awareness of Karma, the Oneness of everything, and Reincarnation. This center will also function at a level that will allow abundance into the lives of those who seek it. Its color is **SILVER**.

(9.) The "HIGHER SELF CHAKRA" ...when activated will bring enlightenment. At its most basic level it provides us with protection. By its ability to transmute any negative energy that enters its realm, we can be kept free from agitating thoughts and disruptive feelings that don't belong to us. This energy can free the person who receives it in miraculous ways by opening doors that were believed to be closed. Its color is **GOLD**.

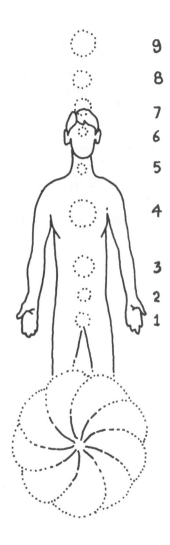

9
8
7
6
5
4
3
2
1

Main Chakra Line-Up.

(1.) Speaking on a subject he knows well, John creates YELLOW for the Crown Chakra. The BLUE of the Throat Chakra reveals the clear and charismatic energy from his speech. And the ORANGE from his shoulders shows us the vitality he's putting into it. CLEAR LIGHT descends from above.

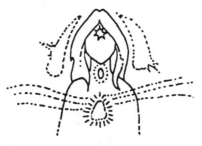

(2.) Mary is feeling heartsick and very depressed over her relationship with her boyfriend. The Heart Chakra feels weighted and is GRAY-RED. (We see the gray-red because that's how we perceive her sadness. Our inner mind relates information to us in a way that we can understand.) A DARK BLUE band flows through the aura. A DARK GREEN shrouds her head and shoulders. The Throat and Third-eye are also discolored. Her outlook is dismal and she feels that the communication lines are down with her boyfriend.

(3.) After a long day, John is mentally and physically spent. BURNT ORANGE drapes his shoulders, and a GRAY YELLOW-GREEN forms a cap over his head at the Crown Chakra. The MUDDY YELLOW circle to his right is stress.

(4.) Here Mary has reached a state of peace with herself and feels very spiritual. Her Chakras are open and flowing well. A bright CRYSTALLINE BLUE bubble surrounds her. Shimmering WHITE LIGHTS dance around the edges.

KNOWING THE DIFFERENCE BETWEEN
FEELING AND SEEING THE AURA

To help you understand the difference between these two senses and how they operate, I've drawn an illustration showing two men. The one on the right is John and he is receiving the other's energy.

John is feeling the aura in the area of his mid-section. Remember the expression, gut feeling? He is receiving a hunch about his associate at the gut level, a kind of knowing. (The Stomach Chakra.) The energy he is receiving with his heart area will help him gain some understanding of the other man. (The Heart Chakra.) It's an emotional reaction. Most men do not open their hearts up to feel this sensing. They work with the intellect, their gut hunches. However, a balanced thinking and feeling man is usually at his best.

These two areas just discussed are the main centers of feeling for the Inner Self. So basically you *feel* on two levels: (1.) A Gut-knowing, or (2.) Understanding.

Besides feeling there is sight. We *see* and gain *insight* from a different sense. This level is the Inner Self's projector. It displays pictures and communicates the impressions John is receiving. John is seeing his associate's aura and what he sees will let him know how the other is receiving his energy and the other's reactions and responses to him.

The combination of both *seeing* and *feeling* presents the best method in reading others. This will help validate what John is picking up. Both senses should say the same thing. If not, reinspection could prove valuable for best results.

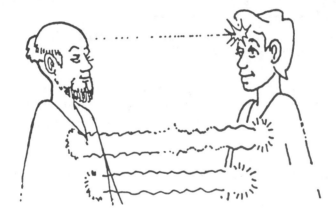

Knowing the difference in Sensing

HOW TO SEE A SPIRIT GUIDE

To see a Spirit Guide takes a good imagination. And there is a reason for this. They are vibrating at a much faster speed making them invisible to us. When we seek to see them, we raise our vibrations. We speed up the light moving within us by raising our consciousness, through meditation and breath. We speed up, they slow down, and we meet halfway. To some this is called the "lifting of the veil."

All things are made up of light, slowed down to form the physical reality. Everything that we can see, feel, and touch is vibrating between 300,000 angstrom units per second to 400,000 angstrom units per second.

(Angstrom: a unit used in measuring the length of light waves.)

As humans, we begin vibrating at about 365,000 angstroms and increase our speed from there. As we master this world, this dimension, we move closer to vibrating at 400,000. I'm told that the last 10,000 units towards 400,000 is a real bear, and that it can take lifetimes to accomplish. Anyway, when you get to that point, the 400,000 mark, you can manifest things out of the air and walk on water. At the 400,000 angstrom units per second mark is the entrance to the fourth dimension, the invisible world of Spirit.

So the Spirit Guides are behind the veil and we are stretching our imagination to see them. This is really the only possible way to approach this subject.

Stretching our imagination with proper breath will raise our consciousness. To the logical mind they won't exist; they are invisible. And when we do see them, it will not be what we expect.

Spirit will not appear in full 3D projection like something in this reality. The mind's eye has to work to pick up anything vibrating faster than this dimension. There are worlds within worlds. Right now people are moving through you from other dimensions, worlds are living and dying all around and through your physical existence, without your apparent recognition. Through lifetimes of work and progression on your part, you have achieved the ability to tune in to this idea. Those in society who have the unfortunate label of being crazy are really tuning in to other realities, while losing touch with this one. They hear voices or experience things others don't.

In workshops and lectures, I ask the audience at this point to imagine someone standing beside me and for them to let the person appear. They can be of either sex, tall or short, young or old, it doesn't matter. You can do this also. Look to the middle of your room right now and imagine.

When I see Spirit Guides, they first appear vaguely to my perception. I feel their presence in the area first. As I do, I begin to look around to see if I can tune in. Once I have a feeling of where they are, I concentrate and focus my attention. The image starts out being just a faint outline and then maybe the face partially shows itself, or I might see the hair color or style of the clothing and no facial descriptions. Little by little, like a jigsaw puzzle, the image of the Spirit takes form. I say little by little, but it happens in seconds. It just takes adjusting. I'll see the eyes and maybe the outline or mass of the person's face, and then that disappears or fades and the body itself is displayed with a shadow face.

It's important to try to remember what you see as it appears, because you may lose it and if you can remember what you saw you can bring back the memory until the Guide is back in your sight.

The Guides usually have something to share, even if it's simply their presence. I'm not what I call clairaudient. That is, words from the other side do not come to me like outside voices, clear and distinct. They are soft and inside my head and sometimes have trouble getting through all the clutter. But when I settle in and center myself the words get clearer. The usual way they communicate with me is with their hands. Whatever they are doing, whatever they are holding in their hands has some relevance to their message. It's up to me to get clear enough to understand. I feel we are all like this, that it only takes playing with our imagination and getting as clear as possible and then we can tune in. Play with this exercise as much as you can. Everyday is best at first. When you do see a Guide, ask for his name and accept anything that comes to you—pops in your mind--and any pictures associated with it. You *are* tuning in when you perform this exercise. Accept this and you'll have great fun and it doesn't matter if it's real or not. It's the practice and the experience of doing it that counts. YES, you will in time become convinced of seeing the other side, but for now why not just play along.

How to see Spirit Guides

SECTION THREE
MOTHER NATURE'S AURAS

PLANTS

ANIMALS

NATURE SPIRITS

CRYSTALS

THE AURAS OF PLANTS

In 1970, a book was published entitled, **Psychic Discoveries Behind The Iron Curtain.** It tells of an experiment by the Soviets and of their interest in psychic phenomena. Along with Kirlian Photography, other discoveries attracted their attention. Quoting from the book on Page 234: "....the Soviets pumped (the author) for details on the surprising work of Cleve Backster that's caused a sensation in America. Backster, owner of the Backster School of Lie Detection of New York and a recognized expert with the polygraph, announced in 1968 that plants have emotions, memory, and E.S.P."

"Throughout years of careful research, Backster found that plants record a measurable reaction on a lie detector when any living thing dies in their presence. Plants seem to recognize their owners and to respond to the thoughts and emotions of people around them. Backster says, 'It seems to indicate some sort of primary perception or consciousness in every living cell.'"

****

So, plants indeed have an aura. A fog-like energy traces an outline two or three inches out from the body of the plant.

The colors of this aura seem to match the same as those of the plant. Mostly what I seem to recognize is the amount of light coming from the plant and its brightness.

The radiance of light from the plant lets me know about its reaction to its surroundings and soil. When I sit and meditate with plants surrounding me, I'm very relaxed and they give beneficial energies to my psychic expressions.

Communicating with growing things can really give me a good perspective and, for those moments, life takes on a spiritual quality unhampered by everyday business.

My work with auras has been centered around people. I have studied only a little about plants, so my knowledge is limited. In my early studies with the aura group, we were taught about plants and were shown their energies. We watched how plants would send and receive energy from other living things. There were always two or three pets in the room because we were at our Teacher's home. There was a Labrador Retriever and two cats. These animals would come in, lie down and hardly move the whole 20 or 30 minutes of the channeling. There was such a soothing energy in the room, invigorating for the mind and inner senses.

The plants would send energy to the animals and accept some back. The Doctor would call our attention to something happening in the room, an energy display, and ask us to please observe the auras of the dog and the potted plant sitting about three feet from each other. As we focused ourselves, slowing our minds, we would begin to see light moving back and forth between them.

We had our study group in the living room of the house and the lights were very low, most of the time a few candles, but we could see well enough. This low lighting helped in seeing, making it easier on the eyes to concentrate for longer periods of time but low lighting is not necessary. It's good when you start, but training outdoors in the light is better as you go along.

I want to share an example with you that helped me prove my ability to see the auras of plants. When I first began working in Los Angeles at the Psychic Fair, a client, after his reading, thought that he might challenge my ability to see if I really could see auras. *His desire was to learn the ability for himself and he was testing me.* We set an appointment for later that day and I met him at his home. Almost immediately after sitting down my client said, "I bought a new plant today and it's in the room. Can you tell me which one it is?" As I looked around the room, I saw that there were probably twenty plants. The majority were bunched up on a long table and some were scattered around the room in pots or hanging from the ceiling. This guy liked plants.

As I looked them over, one in particular stood out from the others. It was sitting on the table close to the middle in the front. The only real difference I could see was that its aura was lighter and brighter than the others. "That's the plant you bought today," I said as I pointed to it. "That's amazing, you really do see auras!" he said. My client was becoming a little more convinced. The plant hadn't had the time to become adjusted with the others. So naturally its aura was different.

You may want to experiment with this exercise by bringing plants together that are not normally in the same environment, outside plants with inside ones or one from a different home than the others.

A light would flare out from the leaf of the plant about 2-3 inches thick and move in a straight line towards the dog. The dog's aura accepted the energy about eight inches out from the body above its back. The funny thing here is that sometimes the dog would return some light to the plant or send it over to one of the group. There was this complete interplay of energy taking place in the room and we could see it.

WORKING WITH YOUR PLANTS

Exchanging energy and communicating with your plants will be very beneficial to their continued growth. To begin working with your plant, project your aura bubble big enough to include the plant so that both of you can be in sync with each other and can send and receive energy back and forth. Always remember that they can feel your energy and thoughts so be in a positive mood and express good thoughts. Ask your plant if it needs anything like water or soil food and expect an immediate answer. You can give your plant a name and play different styles of music for it, or rearrange its location.These and other similar experiments like them have been employed by top researchers in the past with very noticeable results.

THE AURAS OF ANIMALS

As with the aura of his plants, the young man wanted to continue testing my ability and this time asked me about the aura of his cat. His apartment has a patio with windows and a sliding glass door separating it from the house. He kept the food dish for his cat out on the patio and the curtains were open. The cat was lying in the living room in front of the glass looking at his food on the other side. (He had been playing close to the window for a while.) We know how picky cats can be about their food and it's hard to know when they will eat, but this cat, as it lay there, began to generate a ball of orange light right above its head and upper body. I said to my client, "Watch your cat. In a moment he'll get up and want to go out and eat." Sure enough, within seconds, the cat sat up, meowed at us and headed for the door wanting out. He headed straight for the food.

Animals have three levels of energy in their aura: physical, emotional/reactionary, and spiritual. The spiritual aura of an animal is connected to a group soul or group consciousness of the animal kingdom. This group provides instinctual directions. This consciousness is supported by an Angelic Kingdom created especially for their life form. We'll talk more about this later on.

The emotional/reactionary aura acts as the "thinking" level as well. The animal responds to actions and emotional energies. There is a primitive sensing ability that helps the animal to interpret another life form's energy reactions to them. *They sense the other's aura.*

And then of course, the physical aura lets us know about their health and any actions that they have taken, are now experiencing, or will take in the future.

An animal's aura is a quality that is more dense and speckled than that of humans or plants. They will normally use more than three colors with their aura but it's not as bright or subtle as human auras. Also their bubble is closer to the body.

A funny thing about your pets and their auras is that because they love your attention and care, they will create some of the colors you have in your aura, so they can be more like you. Use your imagination and see what colors associate the pet to the owner.

When I approach a dog who is barking and growling at me, I send a soft blue light out to surround him and mentally tell him that everything is all right. More times than not, it works; sometimes it doesn't. But for the times that it does, it sure is worth it.

THE DEVIC KINGDOM

Just on the other side of Reality, as we know it, there exists a realm of Beings that have been created to work with and help the lower levels of consciousness on this planet. Through their help, the plant and animal kingdoms raise their awareness and can proceed up the evolutionary ladder.

We know them by many names: Leprechauns, Gnomes, Fairies, and Little People, to name a few. They are simply Nature Spirits, Spirits that have taken on human characteristics to form their body because they find great humor in our looks. Of course, many of their looks are exaggerated, like big ears or noses, or other body parts. They can be very mischievous and comical. But their sense of duty to their jobs is taken seriously. They help heal and protect those they watch over and guide them to safety when the need arises.

To see them, you want to pay attention in very wooded areas or gardens. As you gaze at the aura of either plant or animal, you may see some small sparkling lights floating closely about. This is how they will look to you at first. Slowly, as your visualization/imaging grows you'll begin to see them with physical form. At that point communication with them is possible, but they are not trusting of humans, so you must be careful not to be too excited or move too fast.

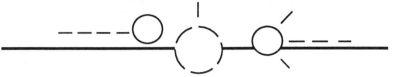

CRYSTALS HAVE AURAS, TOO

Quartz seem to have the easiest auras to
experiment with because they don't have a color to
influence you.

Try holding one and see.
What influence do you sense from it?
And what color is it projecting?
Some even have a taste to them!

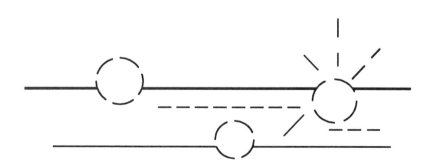

```
┌ ─ ─ ─ ─ ─ ─ ─ ─ ─ ─ ─ ─ ─ ─ ┐
│         SECTION FIVE          │
│  PEOPLE, PLACES, and  THINGS  │
└ ─ ─ ─ ─ ─ ─ ─ ─ ─ ─ ─ ─ ─ ─ ┘
```

THE BUBBLE

SIMPLY OBSERVING

THE AURA OF PLACES

PSYCHOMETRY & HEARING THE AURA

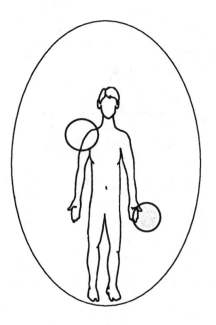

The Bubble

THE BUBBLE

Now that you are aware of the bubble (belonging to the aura, refer to page 17) we will concentrate on it and isolate certain areas that will give more information for your perceptions. With this focus, we again let the first response of our inner self lead the way.

There is no color associated with the bubble in the be-- ginning, only a border/outline which shows us the size and shape to let us tune in. From the bubble we sense density and weight, either lightness and openness, heaviness and restrictions, or anywhere in-between. There may be blocks created in the energy also, from the heaviness and restrictions.

Look at the person and let your focus pick three areas to concentrate on. Find the color that's surrounding the hands. On some occasions each hand will radiate a different color. One hand is receiving energy while the other one can be giving it. Each movement of the hands may change the color. The same applies to the torso and legs. Each of these areas can vibrate different colors simultaneously, which in turn can create different movements of the energy.

With observation, and that's the 'key' word for this exercise, we will expand our ability to tune in to auras at a distance. With me, the distance is as far away as I can see and keep the distinction. Using your ability in this manner provides entertainment. But also it will let you know about a person's energy long before he gets to you. It's like the saying, "I could feel him coming a mile away." It also lets someone spend time seeing auras without being too conspicuous. Most of my observations are usually from twenty or more feet away.

EXERCISE

Go to a public place, a park, beach, river ...any place outdoors where you will encounter animals as well as people. Find yourself a comfortable place to sit.   Close your eyes, and take some slow, deep breaths. Feel yourself becoming centered and surrounded in a bubble (Lavender or Gold, transparent) that will reach ten feet around you. Using a gold triangle with this exercise is also very effective and supplies a tremendous amount of focus towards your power. Now let energy from your Inspirational Aura begin to flow down through your body from the top of your head to the base of your spine, and then back up the front of your body to your 'mind's eye.'

Let the energy rest there a moment or two, and then feel it projecting outward in a clockwise spiral. Let this energy flow easily, don't push.

Open your eyes and begin looking around. Notice someone close by. Imagine the size of the bubble, just imagine. If you have a note pad with you, draw what you see in your mind's eye. Note everything that you pick up and date it. You might want to use the worksheets that are supplied at the back of the book.

PEOPLE

I'm a great people watcher. I love to go to gatherings, indoors and out, and observe people. When I do this I am not intrusive. I don't look for anything except the surface colors and what the energies are doing. I never look for anything that's not available on the surface. I'm there to enjoy myself because it's entertaining, and I'm also practicing. The energy between people can be very funny.

When I'm in my car and stopped at a traffic light, I sometimes see bicyclists pedaling by and I look at their bubbles, noticing the colors around the legs, arms, and torso. I see how the bubble is shaped and how big it is. Sometimes it's shaped oval and leaning forward. But there will be different shapes according to the person's energy while riding. Here is another fun experiment you can try. I'm always on the look-out for a chance and excuse to practice. You may choose to do this while waiting in any line, but be careful not to make it too obvious.

****

There is a very natural occurrence that we involve ourselves with everyday. We give and take with each other, exchanging energy. We pass on thoughts and feelings, likes and dislikes, to others. And when we have the need to energize ourselves, we take energy from someone else.

Like I said, it's quite natural for us to do this. All life forms participate in this. It's what's keeping everything alive. With a good exchange, everything is in balance. And when the exchange is not good, being instead filled with disrupting vibrations, it can effect many things at once. All life forms that come into contact with it can be effected.

A man troubled over his job may create havoc everywhere he turns. Besides his family, the forms of life in and around his home, like the pets and plants, will also feel the brunt of the vibrations. These harsh vibrations do effect animals, we've all seen this, and quite interesting are the experiments with plants seeing how the plants will grow in different environments. Just as you and I, plants and animals like it better when things are pleasant.

In the group we were given the instructions to observe the energy, and we watched how it happened. Most of the exchanges we have with people are taking place on a different level of consciousness. Sometimes we are open to people and sometimes we're not. During those times that we are open, we usually take some of their energy right along with us when we leave. The energy we take may have problems that we are not aware of. Sometimes the person is having a hard time, and we walk away with some of that frustration, pain, or hurt. If they've generated a block in the flow of their energy, we may develop the same.

I've gathered energy subconsciously that has caused me trouble on more than one occasion and I'm sure you have too. But you may have not known about it. I was ignorant of it until it was clearly pointed out. Then it made sense.

One night with the group I asked the Doctor to speak more on observing. I wanted to be more useful in directing the light energies we were coming to know, and I wanted to start doing the work. The Doctor looked at me with that smile of his and then paused and said, "Do not enter into another Being's field of energy. You may cause yourself harm." I discovered later on what the Doctor was saying, because working with the light can often involve entering into another's aura to work on healing.

Of course I said, "Why not?" The Doctor replied, "It is not yet time for you to do your work. But it *is* time to observe. Observe from a distance. You will see many things in your experiments and you will learn by **simply observing**. Focus on the bubble. The thoughts of others belong to them and I am sure that you have your own. Having another Being's thoughts bouncing around with your's can be troublesome." Continuing with his 'looking-right-through-me, knowing-me-better-than-myself', smile, the Doctor said, "You do not wish for this, do you?" "Uh,no..no. Not me! I'm fine like I am."

Did I listen? Or was it that I didn't remember? Anyway, somewhere along the way I thought I was ready, or better than all the stuff I would encounter, and I went diving into the auras of those I thought needed my service, applying light to their problems and blocks, and it did create a lot of problems.

PLACES

Because people give off vibrations, they leave them wherever they spend time in living or working. Have you ever noticed how each family home has its very own feel and smell? It's not always easy to get comfortable in another's home, unless you know them well. The same is true with an office or work area belonging to someone else. Each has his own way of being and that unique presence is left in the air, on the objects within the area, and even in the walls.

Churches can be peaceful and restful and Holy, because that's what people create there. Nightclubs and bars can feel dirty and intimidating. Hospitals can feel very unhealthy because of all the sickness brought into its environment. Again, it all depends on the people and what kind of thoughts and feelings they project while in the area.

I remember once when I was about ten or eleven years old, going into a building that was old and abandoned, an old mechanic's garage. At one point in moving around in the building, I was hit with a strange feeling of dizziness. It lasted a minute or two and then went away. But I knew I got it from the weirdness of the place and from the person who had worked there before it closed. A part of me knew this. That's why I can still recall the event; it felt real scary.

Or how about this? You return home to an empty house only to feel like someone has been there while you were gone. It's happened to me. There was even a faint and brief smell of body odor as I walked up the steps. It wasn't anything noticeable, but my psychic self sensed it. Someone I didn't want to see had dropped by and fortunately I hadn't been home to greet him.

There are places of historical value, where tremendous things occurred. Getting in touch with the vibrations of the spot can be very enlightening.

There have been times when I have gone to sacred areas and got in touch with Spirits. Because different places on the planet are more highly charged than others it is easier to tune in. On Mt. Shasta, I met a Spiritual Teacher, in spirit, who communicated with me. In Hawaii, on the Big Island, at a sacred Heiau, I was easily able to tune in to the Spirit guards protecting the energy. Also in Hawaii, on Oahu, at a place where the battle for the Kingdom occurred, I got in touch with all the trama from the battle and witnessed Spirits who were killed there still hovering above the grounds.

Spirits who loved being where they have once lived will return to visit. Others will leave such a great presence that it will be quite noticeable as you move through the area. All in all, places can and do hold energy and they can be experienced when we are sensitive to them.

THINGS

APPLIED PSYCHOMETRY AND HOW IT CONNECTS WITH THE AURA

Everything that is handled by someone, holds a trace of his vibrations. The emotions and thoughts of that person can be readily perceived by anyone who becomes sensitive to it.

This system of psychic reading is one of the easiest ways to test your ability: Quiet yourself and close your eyes while holding onto an object.

There are materials used to make things that are not conducive to retaining vibrations, i.e., plastics, man-made fabrics. Things that work, are natural, i.e., metals, wood, leather, stone, gems, and all by-products. Good things to hold are keys, jewelry, wallets, and purses.

After a moment or two of concentration on the object you will get impressions about its owner. Some impressions you will feel within and others you will see on your mind's eye. The majority of what you receive will be over 50% accurate on your first few tries.

For best results start to talk about what you're picking up as soon as you pick it up, because by talking about it, the information will *flow* instead of *come and go*. When you get even the slightest impression, say it. This acceptance will move you along the path. And when working with an object, hold it loosely in your hands, shifting it back and forth between them, so you can be comfortable while you focus.

THE SOUND OF THE VIBRATIONS

With this exercise I also want you to try using another one of your senses. I want you to listen to the sound your object makes. You will hear a pitch in your mind, like what you hear in a hearing test. The pitch will tell you how fast the energy of the person is vibrating.

This fun sense of hearing began one night at an impromptu group session. There were six or seven of us hanging out at Diane's new house and wanted to have her sit for us for another talk with the Doctor. But she had been conducting groups two nights a week already and with good heartedness, refused. "Do something on your own. Ask your teacher to give you something to do."

This idea came to me to try hearing the aura. Listening to my guides was new and still rather foreign to me, so I wasn't sure how the idea came, I just thought I'd give it a go.

So I told the others and asked if they wanted to try doing it, and they agreed. We had one person stand across the room from us and we all got quiet and focused our attention on hearing the aura. My impression was immediate and everyone else said the same. We tried next with another person joining the first. The sound changed. The first two were women, so we added a man and the pitch dropped. We put four people up there and then one at a time got them to leave. It was a great experiment. We got them to move as fast as they could back and forth from our group to the gruop across the room. Each time the pitch would change.

When you first begin holding an object that you want to psychometrise, quietly listen to the vibrations. This will give you some clue about the person. You may even hear it wobble. When this happens, there will be changes occurring in the life of the person. But use your own intuitiveness with this exercise and see how accurate you get. It's really fun and a great way to expand your ability.

AND ALSO DON'T FORGET TO RECEIVE A COLOR FOR THE PERSON. THE SOUND CARRIES ITS OWN SPECIAL COLOR.

SECTION SIX

SYMBOLS

and

THOUGHT FORMS

SYMBOLS

A common occurrence when you first begin to look into auras is to see symbols. Symbols refer to single item pictures such as a feather, ball, castle, etc. By that I mean that out of the field of color you see, an object will spring into your perception. It will not be like seeing a complete picture. It is just a symbol ... something to a bigger story. Symbols provide the outer message, a synopsis. They speak of something within or beyond. They are your entry point. And only through practice and inner work will you be able to get beyond the point of symbols. It does take time. For most it takes years.

As we grow and practice this ability, symbols will have more than one item floating about. Pictures will form, but they will just be bigger or more complete symbols and more clues. They will give an ABSTRACT view.

A practicing Psychic who is in the process of developing more of his skill attended the workshop and began to see things almost immediately. What he saw in the first workshop was this: In his view of another participant, he witnessed the picture of a coliseum, to the woman's right. The coliseum began filling up and as it reached its capacity it began to overflow. He sensed that the woman was a part of the coliseum and was being crowded out.

Upon asking for confirmation from the woman about what he saw, she told him, "Over the last two weeks I've had more house guests than normal for the summer and as one guest leaves it seems like there are two more to fill the space."

"Every room and available space in my home is occupied." So in the greater sense of what the psychic saw, he did not see her home but instead, the coliseum. The crowd pouring in were the house guests. And this was viewed to the woman's right or 'the past'.

So, symbols will be lots of fun to play with in your interpretations of what you see. Experiment with friends often. Try not to be sheepish when telling friends what you see as a symbol and the interpretation your inner self gives you. You'll probably see hundreds of symbols as you progress with aura reading. Stay with the symbols, study them, and they'll soon turn to holograms. A hologram is a true picture liking itself to viewing a movie of a situation in which not only do you see people but also their auras.

A great book for symbol study is "Watch Your Dreams" by Ann Rae Colton. This lady is a recognized Western Master of the Etheric. It's a must read that's full of information and wonderful dream symbology interpretations.

THOUGHT FORMS

Thought forms are over-riding emotions, dreams, de-sires, etc., that will overshadow the reality of what is truly happening in the aura. In your reality there may be nothing remarkable happening to bring changes into your life, but you have a wish for something better or even a fear about it and project it out with more power than you normally express. This, then, becomes a large picture or display of energy that stands in front of the more real avenues of your creations.

As an example, I remember on one occasion while read-ing for a friend, I described a home around her which was different from her present one. She and her boyfriend were looking for a home to live in after they were married. I described the home to the letter, complete with landscaping, brickwork, and color.

This is where the idea of the thought form comes into play. As I received the picture, I saw a large projection. The picture took up the area from the shoulder to well below the waist on the left side of my friend's body, the future side. It was very clear and easy to see. I did not fight to bring in the picture's clarity. Sometimes when working with people the picture jumps in and out and takes time to stabilize. But this image appeared readily and without effort. It showed itself at the very beginning of my tuning in.

As I described the house to my friend, her emotional aura began to withdraw and become heavy and I saw that she was upset. "That's the house we saw today and I refuse to move into it. My fiance likes it because it's in good condition, but the rest of the neighborhood is run down. I told him 'no'. That's not the house we're moving into, is it?"

Because I knew the picture to be a thought form, only after sensing her aura and comparing it to the rest of what I saw, was I able to calm her down and really look into her future. In my earlier years with aura reading, thought forms confused the situation and the advice I was giving.

But thought forms are not all bad. They're quite interesting really. I've seen some wild ones that got my attention. And who knows? In the future the new pick-up line may be, "Hey,.. nice thought forms!"

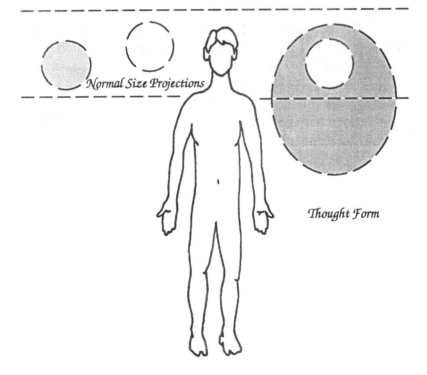

Normal Size Projections

Thought Form

The question is asked during the workshop, "Do we project thought forms around others as well as ourself?"

We answer with, "Yes we do. And many times this energy will be accepted by the other and will have it's influence on him for a few minutes or even a few days. But it doesn't have to be accepted."

Another question is asked, "I've seen symbols and colors around people but how do I know if what I am seeing isn't really 'my' desires and feelings about them? How can I get a fairly accurate reading with someone I know?"

We answer with, "Begin by asking permission from the other person's Higher Self (their creation connection) to look into the aura and also to receive the correct answer to your question. Breathe deeply, center and ground yourself, step away from preconceiving, and then ask. The answer you receive should feel unemotional, clear and unobstructed. But, sometimes Divine Law doesn't allow the answer to be given.

> ## SECTION SEVEN
> ## MEDITATIONS and EXERCISES

MEDITATION

THREE RINGS OF POWER

GENERATING LIGHT, EXERCISES

MEDITATION

I am going to present a small meditation idea to you. I have participated in many group meditations and the ones that impressed me the most used a technique like this.

(1.) Begin by sitting or lying in a comfortable position. Close your eyes and begin breathing in a slow rhythmic pace. Breathe in through the nose to the count of four heartbeats, filling the base of your lungs first, forcing the stomach out and slowly counting to four. Then release the breath through your mouth counting again to four. Do this three or four times. This will slow down your heart rate and relax the mind. Now allow a blank canvas to appear in front of you.

(2.) See in your mind a nice white cloud forming over your head. Let this cloud begin to flow down through your body, filling every cell as it moves toward the bottom of your feet. Let this cloud extend into the ground beneath you and move to the center of the earth, connect, and then return. As it returns, allow this energy to move out from your heart surrounding your body with a bubble that reaches 10 feet in all directions. Now you are ready to begin your visualizations.

ADVANCED MEDITATION

This next exercise was given to me around 1984. It wasn't all given at once, but in pieces. This was because the first part was for stablizing my energies. Later on the rest came as my needs became more conscious. I've learned through practice to be able to perform the technique in a matter of seconds, and let me say that it works and has been invaluable. Most of the time before entering a public area like a shopping mall, or a meeting with a person or group of people, I use it.

The first words of the exercise stated that I should learn to flow with the cosmic energies like a boat upon the sea rolling with the swells but staying in balance.

Each time things around me get out of my control, I think of the little boat on the water and allow myself to flow through the problem of the difficult energies. This would insure balance. As I exercised this, I soon had the impression to begin using the spinning rings. The spinning rings would be stable (like a gyroscope) and I was free to move and bob and roll, within them. The rings would be my protection.

THE THREE RINGS OF POWER

Become still. See with your mind's eye a golden ring of light spinning slowly around your body at the heart's level. Now see another at your knees, and then the third ring orbiting your head just above the eyes.

These rings are orbiting from left to right in a clockwise motion. Now allow the rings to slowly gain momentum in their spin. Above your head is a large white cloud filled with cosmic energy. As the rings spin faster, they will begin to draw the cloud down into their circle and fill the entire area surrounding your body. Breathe in the energy, let it totally engulf you and feel the surge of power. After a brief time when you're feeling good and strong release the image. (Now it's up to you to decide how thick or wide you'd like the rings to be and how far out away from your body they will spin.) This exercise really stablizes and protects me.

The rings may spin opposite or *counter clockwise* when you first begin; let them. The opposite motion is cleaning out any problem energies that have been hanging out around you, pulling the old energy up and out the top of your aura getting you ready to receive the new energy.

The gold is very powerful not by keeping your energy in, but by keeping other's out. I am saying this to let you know that as you awaken to your light within and let it shine out, you will attract those who want it. Some of those will only desire to use it for selfish reasons. Like a moth to a flame, the light attracts. It doesn't discriminate between creative unlimited energies or stagnate ones. Those whose energy is stagnate will leave a residue with you that will disrupt your energy field. That's what I call the dizzies. I have been assualted with energy that has made me dizzy for a time, even sick to my stomach. So the rings of light are my protection.

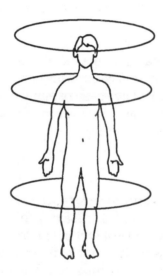

Three Rings of Power

SOME FUN EXERCISES

To help you expand with your inner-perceptions, here are some great exercises that I have learned.

Expand your aura field - make your bubble bigger.

The purpose of this will help you become more aware of how much energy you are projecting. As mentioned before, we normally have our bubble three to six feet out from us.

So, get comfortable, close your eyes, and begin to breathe at a slow rythmic pace. Sense your bubble resting around you at 3 feet. As you breathe, and allow the white light above you to descend into your bubble and move out from your heart or stomach area, imagine that with every breath you are blowing up your bubble like a balloon.

Feel your energy move through objects that are surrounding you. Sense each object as you pass through it. Whether you are inside a dwelling or not, get in touch with those things closest to you.

The more you practice this the bigger you'll get with expanding your aura. Whenever I travel by car, I increase my bubble to 300 yards in all directions, in front, behind, and to the sides of the car. I also expand it over and under the vehicle. This affords me protection from an accident and keeps me in touch with and alert to the other drivers on the road in any of these directions.

Generate a ball of light and send it to a friend.

This is a fun way to send energy without being noticed. You have an imaginary body that is just like your real one. With your eyes open or closed, whichever is easier for you, place your imaginary hands out in front of you a few feet apart with the palms facing each other.

Again breathe and collect energy form the top of your aura and this time allow it to form into a ball in front of you between your hands. You can make this bubble any size you choose – from a baseball to a beachball. Picture in your mind as best you can, the face of the person you wish to send energy to. Ask your psychic self to give you the color it thinks your frined would like the best at the moment. As the ball begins to solidify in-between your hands, add the color.

Now you are free to throw it, kick it, or send it anyway you like. Distance is no obstacle. Watch the ball fly through the air and land on top of your friend and then blend down into his bubble. Think of it as a blessing to energize him, fill him with love, protection, or whatever would be to his own best interest.

I like to use this technique to send energy to people I see that I feel would like some added energy, even if I don't know them. For those times I simply send white light.

I also like to create balls of light and place them touching the ceiling when I'm riding on a bus or sitting in a room with a group of people. I place a color inside the ball and see who takes it into his bubble. Unconsciously, the person will send out a beam of light and connect with the ball and take from it the color and energy he needs. Not everyone does this and it's interesting to see who does.

Generate a bubble and travel to other times and places.

This exercise can take you to past lives as well as let you go to other places on the planet and also to other worlds. It requires a lot of visualization practice and a willing imagination.

To begin, find a quiet place and get comfortable. Do your prep work of breathing and centering. Close your eyes and see your bubble in your mind. Use the color gold. Make sure you leave your bubble transparent. Breathe deeply and reinforce your bubble with power from your stomach chakra.

Now with your breathing, let your bubble become lighter-than-air. Exhaling will be the energy that lightens up your bubble.

As your bubble lightens, you will begin to ascend. Slowly see yourself at tree level and then higher. Look below and see the surrounding city or countryside. You may stay there for a time if it's fun to you. Continue with your climb until you are above the clouds. See the clouds as being a cover between you and the ground – a solid carpet. Now that you are there, ask your Higher Self to place you at the best possible location for your present experience in life, whether a past life, location on the earth, or another planet.

Begin moving forward, speeding up little by little until you are really flying along. Notice the Moon or Sun above. After a short time of flying at high speed, look around for an opening in the clouds. Begin to slow down your bubble as you approach the opening, and then stop right above it. Get yourself ready to descend.

Your bubble will now begin to descend through the clouds, and as it does, if you can, notice what's beneath you. It's quite alright if you don't. You may descend quickly if you like. Once you land, stand up and move out of your bubble and look around. If you're having trouble visualizing, look down at your feet and see if you are wearing footware and what it is. This will usually help you begin your journey.

If it's possible, you should have a friend take you through this meditation. That friend should begin asking you questions, such as; "What is around you? Do you see any people? Who are they? " and so on. If you are traveling to see a past life, they should ask, "How old are you? Where do you live? Do you see parents or relatives belonging to that lifetime?" and so on. Questions are important and always the most detailed will help you tune in with what you are visualizing. I suggest that you first ask the age of who you are in that lifetime then move directly forward or back to the age of five years old. From that point, move forward five years at a time until that lifetime is over. Stay emotionally detached at all times so that death or other problems will not affect you.

I suggest that you don't spend longer than twenty minutes on your journey. When it's time, go back to your bubble and return to the present by going in reverse until you are back to your present location. Once there, you may move back to consciousness by counting slowly from 1 to 10. When you reach the count of ten you will be wide awake, feeling good, and remembering all that took place.

So, Good Luck and Bon Voyage!

JOURNAL
QUESTIONS and WORKSHEETS

1. What was your first impression of your subject's aura?

2. How big was the bubble?

3. What was the strongest color or feeling you received from the aura?

4. How many colors did you receive altogether?

5. What did you feel about your subject? Was the aura comfortable to your senses? Was it heavy or light or just right?

6. Were you able to observe the aura change color or energy movement? Explain.

7. How much time did you spend with the reading?

8. Were you able to get confirmation on what you received from your subject's energy? List your 'hits'.

9. Did you pick-up any symbols/pictures?

10. Did you get a sense of timing with what you received?

11. Were you able to divide the levels of the aura, as you looked into the bubble?

12. Did you see any Spirits surrounding your subject? Did you sense them to be Teachers, Guides, Friends or Relatives?

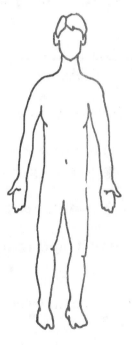

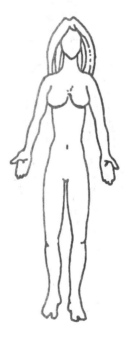

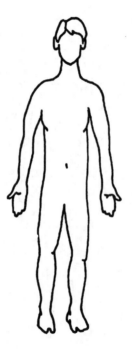

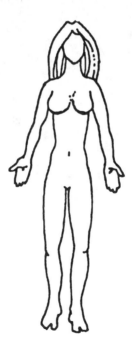

JOURNAL